mudpuppy

f ⓘ @mudpuppykids

Design © Mudpuppy | www.mudpuppy.com
70 West 36th Street New York, NY 10018

Illustrations © Lydia Ortiz & Patrick Rafanan
Text by Yelena Moroz Alpert

Designed in the U.S.A. | Manufactured in China
Printed with soy-based inks.

Little FEMINIST

CELEBRATING 25 *amazing* WOMEN THROUGHOUT HISTORY

Words: **YELENA MOROZ ALPERT**
Pictures: **LYDIA ORTIZ & PATRICK RAFANAN**

mudpuppy

CLEOPATRA

Cleopatra may have lived more than 2,000 years ago, but her reign as the last queen of Egypt is not forgotten.

It wasn't only Cleopatra's beauty and gold that made her powerful. She was creative, clever, and knew how to get things done!

When plotting to capture the Egyptian throne, Cleopatra wanted the Roman emperor, Julius Caesar, to be on her side. But there was one problem: she wasn't allowed to see him. Did Cleopatra complain? No. She wrapped herself in a rug and had it delivered to him in secret! The emperor was so impressed with this sneaky trick that he agreed to help her become Egypt's queen.

Cleopatra went on to rule the richest kingdom in the world for more than 20 years. People called her the Queen of Kings and treated her like a goddess.

Queen Elizabeth I

When Queen Elizabeth I was born, her father was disappointed. He wanted a son to rule England, just like him. Four hundred years ago, people thought women couldn't make great rulers, but Elizabeth was a natural leader and proved them all wrong!

Rich and famous men wanted to marry her, but Elizabeth chose to rule without a king. As queen, she brought peace to her country. People were happy and spent this time writing entertaining plays and composing beautiful music.

Years later, the king of Spain wanted to take over England, but Elizabeth said, "No way!" Even though Elizabeth's navy had fewer ships, they defeated their enemy during a big sea battle. This victory made England the ruler of the seas for hundreds of years.

SACAGAWEA

Two hundred years ago, the path to the Pacific Ocean wasn't mapped, but explorers Meriwether Lewis and William Clark changed that. They traveled from Missouri to Oregon thanks to one very important person: Sacagawea, a 16-year-old Native American girl.

Over 18 long months, Sacagawea helped make trade deals with Native American tribes and found edible roots and berries when there was no other food. She even saved the whole Lewis and Clark expedition by rescuing important supplies when a canoe tipped over in the middle of a river. Sacagawea did all this while caring for her baby boy, who was strapped to her back during the 3,700-mile journey!

Sacagawea's bravery was not forgotten. Dozens of American parks and rivers are named in her honor and her face appears on the gold dollar coin.

Harriet Tubman

Harriet Tubman was born into slavery—she was not free. Once she escaped enslavement, her mission was to help others find their freedom too.

Harriet was put to work when she was just 5 years old. When she grew up, she ran away through the Underground Railroad, a network of secret trails that led slaves to places where they could be free. It was very dangerous, and if she was caught, she would have been beaten, or worse! The people who helped slaves find their way to safety were called conductors, and they helped Harriet make her getaway.

Once Harriet was free, she became a conductor too. For more than 10 years, she guided over 300 slaves to freedom through swamps and dark forests. Harriet became one of the bravest conductors of the Underground Railroad.

⇒ MARIE CURIE ⇐

Scientist Marie Curie was studying radioactivity (how objects give off energy) when she discovered two new chemical elements.

One night, she walked into her lab and saw a mysterious silvery light. The powder from her experiment glowed—it was the new metal that Marie was looking for! Marie named it radium because it looked like a ray of light. Radium is now used by doctors to treat diseases like cancer.

Marie also discovered another element, polonium, named for her native country Poland. Polonium can power space satellites orbiting Earth.

Marie was the first person in history to receive two Nobel Prizes for her scientific discoveries, one in physics and one in chemistry. More than 100 years later, Marie is still the only woman to accomplish this extraordinary feat.

AMELIA EARHART

No adventure was too big for thrill-seeking pilot Amelia Earhart. She wanted to break flight records for speed and distance, just like men.

Once Amelia decided she was going to fly, nothing could stop her. She loved flying so much that she worked several jobs to buy her own little plane—The Canary! Amelia's hard work paid off and she became the first woman to fly over the Atlantic Ocean, first as a passenger, then on her own.

Still, she dreamed of flying around the world. This would be her last and most difficult challenge. On her journey, she glided over wild jungles in South America, saw hippos in Africa, and soared next to eagles in India. Amelia flew more than 20,000 miles. Her trip was almost complete when her plane disappeared over the Pacific Ocean. Amelia was never found, but her spirit for adventure lives on.

FRIDA KAHLO

Before Frida Kahlo, no woman painted her feelings so honestly. But Frida's story of becoming one of Mexico's most famous artists began with an accident.

When Frida was a teenager, she was in a terrible bus crash that changed her life. She broke many bones and had to stay in bed for months. To pass the time, Frida started painting self-portraits. She never stopped.

She painted herself with her beloved pet monkeys and parrots when she felt happy, and she painted herself in pain when she felt sad. While her colorful art might look like a strange dream, to Frida, it was the world as she saw it.

No matter what, Frida always said *Viva la vida!* It means "live life," and that is exactly what she did with her art.

Josephine Baker

Josephine Baker showed the world that black women are beautiful and glamorous. Even her pet leopard, Chiquita, wore a diamond collar!

Josephine grew up poor in St. Louis, but her dancing made her a superstar in Paris. There, people didn't care that Josephine was black. They loved her lively shows and outrageous costumes. But things were different in America. Her Broadway co-stars ignored her and hotels made her use the back door.

Josephine didn't think this treatment was fair, so she stood up for herself and people like her. At the famous March on Washington, she spoke about equality alongside Martin Luther King, Jr. Josephine believed that everyone was created equal, no matter what they looked like.

GEORGIA O'KEEFFE

When Georgia O'Keeffe painted, she transformed an ordinary object into something special.

Georgia painted flower petals so large, they took up the entire canvas. Her paintbrush worked like a magnifying glass, showing details people had not noticed before.

As Georgia grew older, she fell in love with the open land of New Mexico and made the state her adopted home. There, she painted the redness of the mountains and the beautiful shapes of animal bones found scattered throughout the desert.

By the time Georgia was 98 years old, she had painted almost 1,000 pictures of flowers, landscapes, and even skulls. Her work made her the leader of a new art style called American Modernism.

ROSA PARKS

Rosa Parks was tired of segregation (the act of keeping white and black people separate)—so she did something about it!

In the 1950s, black people had to sit at the back of the bus, but white people could sit anywhere. It was the law. One day, a bus driver told Rosa to get up so a white man could sit in her place. She did not move. For this, the police came and took her to jail.

But Rosa wasn't scared to fight for what's right. She worked with her friend Martin Luther King, Jr. to end this unjust law. They told black people in their community to stop riding buses until they had the same rights as white bus riders. Because of Rosa's bravery, the Supreme Court changed the law and said that everyone who rode the bus could sit where they chose.

Katherine Johnson

A man may have walked on the moon, but it was a woman who helped put him there—her name was Katherine Johnson. Before computers, NASA, the American space program, counted on people like Katherine to solve difficult mathematical problems.

Katherine could predict where a spaceship would land by calculating its speed and the moon's orbit. Unfortunately, not everyone saw her brilliance right away—she lived at a time when women and black people were often overlooked.

But Katherine knew her work was important. She spent several years working out math problems to make sure the Apollo 11 spaceship landed on the moon *and* carried the astronauts safely back to Earth. Thanks to Katherine, the American space program really took off!

LOUISE BOURGEOIS

For the French-American artist, Louise Bourgeois, art was a tool for sharing feelings. For example, when Louise became frustrated with working while taking care of her family, she painted houses (not heads!) on top of women's shoulders.

Louise made art using unique materials like nightgowns, cages, and jagged wood. One of her most famous sculptures is a gigantic steel spider called *Maman*—it means Mommy in French. Some people may think a spider is scary, but to Louise, it was a symbol of love for her mother who was clever, creative and very good at weaving.

Louise worked for almost 70 years and made hundreds of paintings, sculptures, and prints. Although her art wasn't always easy to understand, Louise didn't mind—it made people think differently, especially about women.

WILMA ★ RUDOLPH

Wilma Rudolph's nickname was the Black Gazelle—she was the fastest female runner in the world! But Wilma didn't always run fast. In fact, as a little girl, she could barely walk. When she was 4 years old, she got sick and one of her legs stopped working. Wilma hated wearing her metal leg brace because it kept her from playing sports. She was determined to get it off by doing special exercises.

Not only did Wilma recover, but she became a high school basketball star who dashed across the court as fast as lightning. A track coach saw her speedy moves and offered her a spot on a college track team.

Before long, Wilma won three gold medals at the 1960 Olympic Games in Rome—a first for an American woman. She sprinted 100 meters in just 11 seconds, proving that champions can overcome anything!

Ella Fitzgerald

Ella Fitzgerald was the Queen of Jazz. Her silky voice could transform any song into unbelievable music. She also liked to play with sounds, like "dubi-dubi-doo-wop." This singing style is called scatting. When she sang like that, her voice mimicked instruments, like trumpets and trombones.

Before Ella became famous, she danced and sang on the streets of New York City. She didn't have clean clothes and her hair was messy, but that didn't stop her from winning first place at the famous Apollo Theater's talent night. Soon, she was the star of her own jazz band.

Ella's voice was magical and people couldn't get enough. She recorded song after song—selling more than 40 million albums! She was the first black woman to win a Grammy, the top music honor, and she went on to win 12 more. Ella showed that greatness has no limits.

GLORIA STEINEM

Gloria Steinem gave women a voice. She did this by first listening to what women had to say—no matter if they were from India or Indiana.

When she started working as a journalist in the 1950s, male writers didn't take women's ideas seriously. But Gloria thought it was important to hear women's opinions about family life, government, and world events. She traveled all over America writing news stories, giving speeches, and organizing groups that fought for equal treatment of women and men.

At first, she was nervous to talk in front of a crowd, but with the help of her friends, she became the leader of the Women's Movement. Gloria's voice was loud enough for everyone to hear that women are important.

MAYA LIN

Maya Lin is a famous artist-architect who explores how nature and art come together. Today, her innovative designs are loved by many, but her first big project wasn't understood right away.

Maya was just a college student when she won a competition to design the Vietnam Veterans Memorial, a place to remember soldiers who died in the Vietnam War. Maya's idea was very different from other memorials. Its shiny walls were like black mirrors that reflected the visitors and the Washington, D.C., park where it would be built.

Some people didn't know what to think about her vision, but Maya defended her work. She thought her design would help visitors feel closer to the soldiers who were lost during the war. Because Maya believed in herself, and her ideas, other people did too.

JANE GOODALL

Jane Goodall always loved animals. Her dream was to study wild animals in Africa and she did just that. Jane was the first person to observe chimpanzees in the wilderness.

She bravely hiked the forest alone, looking for chimp families. At first, they were scared of her, but Jane didn't give up. After many months she gained the chimps' trust and was able to feed them bananas by hand!

Some scientists thought her research methods were unusual. Jane believed they worked, and she became a famous chimp expert who showed the world that chimps have personalities and use tools, just like people. She proved that doing things your own way can lead to great discoveries.

JUNKO ❄ TABEI

Junko Tabei was the first woman to stand on top of Mount Everest, the tallest mountain in the world!

When Junko was 10 years old, she hiked her first mountain and loved it. She kept climbing snow-capped mountains all over Japan, where she lived. As Junko grew, she longed for even more adventure and set her sights on Mount Everest. Junko knew she could conquer Everest's steep rocks, freezing winds, and icy ridges.

Junko set off with her all-woman team, the Ladies Climbing Club. Along the way, an avalanche buried her under the snow. She had to be pulled out by her ankles! Still, she continued climbing.

Junko never stopped reaching for the top, scaling the highest peaks in more than 70 countries.

BILLIE JEAN KING

Women had been playing tennis for almost 100 years before tennis champ Billie Jean King fought for respect and equal prize money in tennis tournaments.

When Billie Jean first started playing tennis in the 1960s, men could win a lot more money than women. Billie Jean thought that wasn't fair, so she started a women-only tennis tour with eight amazing players. It was a success! Billie Jean convinced the U.S. Open, a major tennis competition, to award the same amount of prize money to both men and women tennis champions.

Then, Bobby Riggs, a hotshot tennis player, challenged Billie Jean to a match. He thought women were only good at housework and there was no way Billie Jean could beat him in tennis. Billie Jean won and proved him (and his fans) wrong—women can be great at anything!

Ruth Bader Ginsburg

Ruth Bader Ginsburg may not look tough, but her support for equality between men and women has made her a giant.

Even as one of the brightest students in law school, Ruth struggled to find a job as a lawyer after graduation. Sixty years ago, law firms rarely hired women attorneys. Instead, Ruth worked as a law professor, but she was paid less than the male professors at the same university. Ruth set out to change that, and much more.

As a director of the Women's Rights Project, Ruth won lawsuits that changed unjust laws toward women. She was so good at her job that Bill Clinton, the president of the United States, chose her to be a justice on the Supreme Court, the highest court in the country. Since then, Ruth has been deciding some of the most important cases in history. Every day, her work continues to better the lives of millions.

As the first American woman in space, astronaut Sally Ride inspired thousands of people to reach for the stars.

Sally was studying physics when the American space program, NASA, was looking for new astronauts. Women could apply for the first time and Sally thought, "Why not me?"

After five years of training—flying super-fast jets and memorizing the spaceship's computer systems—Sally blasted off in the space shuttle *Challenger*. She spent six days orbiting the Earth and even released a satellite with a robotic arm that she helped build.

Sally loved being an astronaut, but she also loved teaching. When Sally retired from NASA, she and her partner started a program called Sally Ride Science to help kids (especially girls!) see that science, technology, engineering, and math are out of this world.

Maya Angelou

Storyteller Maya Angelou had a way with words. She was a woman of many talents—author, poet, playwright, singer, dancer, actor, and activist—who turned her life's challenges into stories of triumph.

Maya was attacked when she was just 7 years old. Terrified by what happened to her, she refused to say a word for five years. Instead, she kept a journal and read book after book. She noticed that stories sounded better read aloud, and so, she chose to speak again.

As Maya grew up, her voice grew too. She went on to write more than 30 books, including several about her life and difficult childhood. Her stories and poems made people feel that their own stories were important too. Maya's honest words gave people courage to overcome tough times.

Hillary Clinton

Hillary Clinton was the *first* first lady to become a senator and the first woman to run for president of the United States with the support of a major political party.

Hillary was no ordinary president's wife. With her own office inside the White House, she worked nonstop to help poor families, children, and women. She traveled the globe to share her message: "Women's rights are human rights."

She continued to work in government and later became secretary of state. Hillary traveled to 112 countries to meet with leaders and build friendships between America and other nations.

In 2016, Hillary ran for president! While she didn't win the election, almost 66 million people voted for her. Hillary paved a path for other women to follow so that, one day soon, there will be a female president in America.

Misty Copeland

Misty Copeland made way for a new generation of ballerinas. She was the first black principal dancer—the star—at the famous American Ballet Theatre.

Even though she didn't start ballet lessons until she was 13 years old, she learned quickly and soon danced as Clara in *The Nutcracker*. Young Misty was very talented, but with her dark skin, she felt out of place with the other ballerinas. She also worried that her muscular body made her look more like an athlete than a graceful dancer.

But it was Misty's strength that helped her jump higher and twirl faster. By learning to embrace her special gifts, she rose to the top. Misty inspired girls around the world to celebrate their uniqueness.

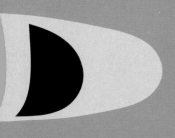

MALALA YOUSAFZAI

Malala Yousafzai loves to learn and believes that all girls deserve an education.

When Malala was an 11-year-old living in Pakistan, a group of men called the Taliban closed all the schools for girls. The Taliban wanted girls to stay home and stop studying. Malala knew this was wrong, so she wrote articles and spoke to reporters about what was happening in her country. This made the Taliban angry and they attacked Malala. She was in the hospital for months, but that didn't stop her from standing up to these bullies.

Malala continued to support girls' right to an education and, together with her dad, she started an organization that helps girls around the world go to school. Malala was just 17 years old when she became the youngest person in history to receive the Nobel Peace Prize.

CLEOPATRA
(69–30 BCE)

AMELIA EARHART
(1897–1937)

KATHERINE JOHNSON
(1918–)

MAYA LIN
(1959–)

SALLY RIDE
(1951–2012)

QUEEN ELIZABETH I
(1533–1603)

FRIDA KAHLO
(1907–1954)

LOUISE BOURGEOIS
(1911–2010)

JANE GOODALL
(1934–)

MAYA ANGELOU
(1928–2014)

SACAGAWEA
(1788–1812)

JOSEPHINE BAKER
(1906–1975)

WILMA RUDOLPH
(1940–1994)

JUNKO TABEI
(1939–2016)

HILLARY CLINTON
(1947–)

HARRIET TUBMAN
(1820–1913)

GEORGIA O'KEEFFE
(1887–1986)

ELLA FITZGERALD
(1917–1996)

BILLIE JEAN KING
(1943–)

MISTY COPELAND
(1982–)

MARIE CURIE
(1867–1934)

ROSA PARKS
(1913–2005)

GLORIA STEINEM
(1934–)

RUTH BADER GINSBURG
(1933–)

MALALA YOUSAFZAI
(1997–)